While every precaution has been taken in the preparation of this book, the publisher assumes no responsibility for errors or omissions, or for damages resulting from the use of the information contained herein.

STRANGE FACTS AND WONDERS

First edition. April 27, 2023.

Copyright © 2023 Kobus Fourie.

ISBN: 979-8223031437

Written by Kobus Fourie.

Table of Contents

Strange Facts and Wonders

Uncovering the World's Strangest Facts

BY

Kobus Fourie

ACKNOWLEDGMENTS

I AM DEEPLY GRATEFUL to the incredible individuals who played a vital role in the creation of this book, and I would like to express my sincere appreciation for their invaluable contributions. Their collective efforts, whether in the form of research, feedback, or unwavering support, have made this project possible, and I am forever indebted to them.

I would also like to extend my heartfelt thanks to the numerous authors, scientists, historians, and experts whose relentless dedication to uncovering and sharing fascinating facts has been the driving force behind this book. Their unwavering passion for knowledge and their commitment to discovery have enriched our world in immeasurable ways, and I am humbled to have drawn inspiration from their profound work.

Lastly, I want to emphasize the significance of curiosity and the joy of learning. This book stands as a testament to the power of embracing one's innate curiosity and the endless possibilities that arise when we seek knowledge. It is my sincerest hope that the pages within these covers will ignite a sense of wonder in readers, encouraging them to venture into the strange and wonderful world that surrounds them. May this book inspire a thirst for exploration and the boundless rewards that come with the pursuit of knowledge.

With deepest gratitude,
Kobus Fourie

Strange facts about Birds

1. A group of penguins in the water is called a "raft" while a group on land is called a "waddle."
2. The smallest bird in the world is the bee hummingbird, which is only 2.25 inches long.
3. The kiwi bird is the only bird with nostrils at the end of its beak.
4. The only bird that can fly backwards is the hummingbird.
5. The ostrich is the largest bird in the world and can run up to 43 miles per hour.
6. The Andean condor has the largest wingspan of any bird, reaching up to 10 feet.
7. The hoatzin bird, found in South America, has a unique digestive system that produces a foul smell resembling cow manure.
8. The male frigatebird has a red throat pouch that it inflates to attract a mate.
9. The kakapo, a parrot native to New Zealand, is the only flightless parrot in the world.
10. The wandering albatross can travel up to 10,000 miles in a single journey, the longest migration of any bird.
11. The only bird known to hibernate is the common poorwill, found in North and South America.
12. The European robin has been known to use discarded cigarette butts to line its nests, as the chemicals in the butts act as a natural insect repellent.
13. The African grey parrot is considered one of the most intelligent birds, capable of learning and using human words and phrases.
14. The male superb lyrebird, found in Australia, is known

for its impressive courtship display where it imitates the sounds of other birds, animals, and even human-made noises.

15. The bar-headed goose is capable of flying over the Himalayan mountains, the tallest mountain range in the world.

16. The shoebill stork, found in East Africa, has a distinctive shoe-shaped bill and is sometimes referred to as the "clown of the swamp."

17. The male satin bowerbird, found in Australia, builds elaborate bowers (or display areas) using a variety of objects to attract a mate.

18. The male peacock is known for its colorful and impressive tail feathers, which can reach up to 6 feet in length.

19. The kea, a parrot found in New Zealand, is known for its mischievous behavior and has been known to steal items such as cameras and car keys from tourists.

20. The barn owl has the ability to hunt in complete darkness thanks to its keen sense of hearing, which allows it to locate prey solely by sound.

<u>Strange facts about War's</u>

1. During World War II, the United States considered using bats equipped with incendiary devices as a weapon to set Japanese cities on fire.

2. The first bomb dropped during World War II landed on a small town in Germany called Freiburg im Breisgau. However, the bomb was actually dropped by accident by a German plane that was returning from a bombing run in France.

3. In 1961, there was a "war" between Honduras and El Salvador that was sparked by a soccer game. The conflict, known as the "Football War," lasted for four days and resulted in around 2,000 deaths.

4. During the American Civil War, a group of soldiers attempted to launch a hot air balloon filled with explosives over Confederate lines. However, the balloon ended up getting caught in a tree and the plan failed.

5. The Soviet Union and Japan never signed a peace treaty after World War II, which means that the two countries are technically still at war.

6. During World War I, the Ottoman Empire recruited German engineers to construct a railroad that would connect Istanbul to Baghdad. This railroad, known as the Berlin-Baghdad Railway, was never completed due to the outbreak of the war.

7. The United States and Canada went to war in 1839 over a disputed boundary in Maine. The conflict, known as the Aroostook War, lasted for several months but resulted in no casualties.

8. During World War II, the United States developed a plan to create a fake army made up of inflatable tanks and other equipment in order to deceive German spies.

9. The Falklands War between Argentina and the United Kingdom in 1982 was sparked by Argentina's invasion of the Falkland Islands, which are located off the coast of Argentina but are a British territory.

10. The Battle of Stalingrad during World War II was one of the bloodiest battles in history, with an estimated 2

million total casualties.

11. The Hundred Years' War between England and France actually lasted for 116 years, from 1337 to 1453.

12. During World War II, the United States conducted experiments on its own soldiers to test the effects of mustard gas and other chemical weapons.

13. The Soviet Union and Finland went to war in 1939 over a disputed border region. The conflict, known as the Winter War, lasted for several months and resulted in around 25,000 Finnish deaths.

14. During World War I, the British army developed a new weapon called the "tanks" to break through enemy lines. The name "tank" was chosen to disguise the true nature of the weapon from enemy spies.

15. The War of the Bucket, fought between the Italian city-states of Bologna and Modena in 1325, was sparked by a dispute over a stolen bucket.

16. During the Vietnam War, the United States used a variety of tactics to try to defeat the Viet Cong, including dropping millions of leaflets from airplanes urging the enemy to surrender.

17. The Boer War, fought between the British Empire and the Boer states in South Africa from 1899 to 1902, saw the first use of concentration camps to imprison civilians.

18. During World War II, the United States developed a program called Operation Paperclip to recruit German scientists, many of whom had worked on the V-2 rocket program, to work for the U.S. military.

19. The Gulf War, fought between a coalition led by the

United States and Iraq in 1991, saw the first use of drones in combat.

20. During the Korean War, the United States developed a plan to use atomic bombs against North Korea and China, but

Strange facts about Towns

1. The town of Hell, Michigan, has a population of only about 70 people, but it attracts tourists with its ominous name and fiery landscape.
2. The town of Colma, California, has a dead population that outnumbers the living population by nearly 1,000 to 1.
3. The town of Coober Pedy in South Australia is known as the "opal capital of the world" and many of its

residents live in underground homes to escape the intense heat.

4. The town of Poveglia in Italy is considered one of the most haunted places in the world due to its history as a quarantine station and mental hospital.

5. The town of Centralia, Pennsylvania, has been burning since 1962 due to an underground coal fire, and it's estimated that the fire may continue burning for another 250 years.

6. The town of Hashima Island in Japan, also known as "Battleship Island," was once a thriving coal mining town but is now abandoned and considered one of the creepiest places on Earth.

7. The town of Whittier, Alaska, has only one building that serves as both the post office, police station, and city hall, among other things.

8. The town of Oymyakon in Russia is known as the coldest inhabited place on Earth, with temperatures regularly dropping to -50 degrees Celsius (-58 degrees Fahrenheit).

9. The town of Roswell, New Mexico, gained fame for the alleged UFO crash that occurred there in 1947, and it has since become a hub for UFO enthusiasts.

10. The town of La Rinconada in Peru is the highest human settlement in the world, with an elevation of over 16,700 feet.

11. The town of Shirakawa-go in Japan is known for its traditional thatched-roof houses, which have been designated a UNESCO World Heritage site.

12. The town of Pripyat in Ukraine, which was once home

to over 50,000 people, has been abandoned since the Chernobyl disaster in 1986 and is now a ghost town.

13. The town of Ostrava in the Czech Republic has been named the European Capital of Culture for 2021, despite being known for its industrial past.

14. The town of Sintra in Portugal is home to several stunning palaces and castles, including the colorful Pena Palace and the mysterious Quinta da Regaleira.

15. The town of Chefchaouen in Morocco is known for its blue-painted buildings and narrow streets, making it a popular destination for photographers.

16. The town of Riomaggiore in Italy is one of the five towns that make up the Cinque Terre region, and its colorful buildings are perched precariously on the cliffs overlooking the Mediterranean Sea.

17. The town of Ísafjörður in Iceland has installed several 3D painted crosswalks to make the town's streets safer for pedestrians.

18. The town of Kowloon Walled City in Hong Kong, which was once the most densely populated place on Earth, was demolished in the 1990s but still holds a fascination for many people.

19. The town of Himeji in Japan is home to Himeji Castle, which is considered one of the most beautiful and well-preserved castles in Japan.

20. The town of Vigan in the Philippines is known for its well-preserved Spanish colonial architecture and is a UNESCO World Heritage site.

<u>Strange facts about Weather</u>

1. The hottest temperature ever recorded on Earth was 134 degrees Fahrenheit in Death Valley, California, in 1913.
2. The highest ever recorded wind speed was 231 miles per hour during Cyclone Olivia in 1996.
3. The deadliest tornado in U.S. history, known as the

Tri-State Tornado, traveled over 200 miles across three states in 1925 and killed 695 people.

4. The world's largest hailstone ever recorded fell in Vivian, South Dakota, in 2010, weighing in at 1.94 pounds and measuring 8 inches in diameter.

5. The heaviest rainfall ever recorded in a single day was 71.8 inches in Foc-Foc, La Reunion, on March 15-16, 1952.

6. The rare phenomenon known as "thundersnow" occurs when thunder and lightning happen during a snowstorm.

7. The wettest place on Earth is Mawsynram, India, which receives an average of 467 inches of rain per year.

8. The driest place on Earth is the Atacama Desert in Chile, where some areas have never recorded any rainfall at all.

9. The largest tornado ever recorded was 2.6 miles wide and traveled for over 100 miles in Oklahoma in 2013.

10. The "fire tornado" phenomenon occurs when a tornado passes over a wildfire, creating a swirling vortex of flames.

11. The "green flash" is a rare optical phenomenon that occurs at sunset or sunrise, when a green spot is briefly visible above the sun's upper rim.

12. The "Sundog" is another optical phenomenon that appears as bright spots on either side of the sun, caused by the reflection of sunlight off of ice crystals in the atmosphere.

13. The "morning glory" cloud is a rare meteorological

phenomenon that occurs in Northern Australia, where long, cylindrical clouds can stretch for up to 600 miles.

14. The "dust devil" is a small whirlwind that occurs on clear, sunny days and is caused by hot air rising from the ground.

15. The "black blizzard" was a severe dust storm that struck the Great Plains of the U.S. in the 1930s, causing widespread crop failures and leading to the displacement of thousands of people.

16. The "Mars dust devil" is a large, swirling dust storm that can stretch up to 12 miles high on the surface of Mars.

17. The "Nor'easter" is a type of winter storm that is known for its strong winds, heavy snow, and coastal flooding along the northeastern coast of the U.S.

18. The "polar vortex" is a large, low-pressure system that occurs in the Arctic and Antarctic regions and can cause extreme cold weather conditions in other parts of the world.

19. The "oceanic pole of inaccessibility" is the point in the ocean that is farthest from any land, located in the South Pacific and known for its unpredictable weather conditions.

20. The "thunderstorm asthma" phenomenon occurs when a thunderstorm causes pollen grains to rupture and release their allergenic particles, leading to severe asthma attacks in susceptible individuals.

<u>Strange facts about Eating</u>

1. The world's oldest piece of chewing gum is over 9,000 years old, made from birch bark tar by ancient people in Finland.

2. In Japan, they have a traditional dish called "fugu," which is made from the poisonous pufferfish. Chefs must undergo extensive training to learn how to safely prepare it.

3. The "Hákarl" is a traditional Icelandic dish made from

fermented shark meat, which is considered a delicacy in the country.

4. In some parts of China, they eat "century eggs," which are made by preserving duck, chicken, or quail eggs in a mixture of clay, ash, salt, quicklime, and rice straw for several months.

5. In many countries, including the U.S., it is common to eat fried insects as a snack, such as crickets, grasshoppers, and mealworms.

6. In Mexico, they have a traditional drink called "pulque," made from the fermented sap of the agave plant.

7. The "Balut" is a popular snack in the Philippines, made from a fertilized duck egg that is boiled and eaten with salt or vinegar.

8. In some African countries, they eat "mopane worms," which are the larvae of the Emperor moth, and are considered a rich source of protein.

9. In Peru, they have a traditional dish called "Cuy," which is made from roasted guinea pig.

10. In some parts of China, they eat "snake soup," which is made from various types of snakes and is believed to have medicinal properties.

11. "Escamoles" are a traditional Mexican dish made from the edible larvae and pupae of ants.

12. In some parts of Africa, they eat "bushmeat," which refers to the meat of wild animals, including monkeys, chimpanzees, and even elephants.

13. In some parts of Southeast Asia, they eat "durian," a fruit known for its pungent smell and custard-like

texture.

14. "Rocky Mountain Oysters" are a dish popular in Western U.S. states, made from deep-fried bull or buffalo testicles.
15. In some parts of the world, they eat "haggis," a traditional Scottish dish made from sheep's heart, liver, and lungs, mixed with oatmeal and spices.
16. In some parts of the world, they eat "black pudding," a sausage made from pig's blood, oatmeal, and spices.
17. In some parts of Africa, they eat "termites," which are considered a delicacy and can be eaten raw or cooked.
18. In some parts of Asia, they eat "bird's nest soup," made from the nests of swiftlets, which are built using their saliva.
19. In some parts of the world, they eat "frog legs," which are considered a delicacy and are often served with garlic and butter.
20. "Fried brain sandwiches" are a traditional dish in some parts of the U.S., made from breaded and fried calf brains.

Strange facts about Bomb's

1. The world's largest man-made explosion prior to the development of atomic bombs was the Halifax Explosion in 1917, which was caused by a collision between two ships carrying explosives in the Halifax Harbour in Canada.

2. The largest nuclear explosion ever recorded was the Tsar Bomba, a hydrogen bomb detonated by the Soviet Union in 1961, with an estimated yield of 50 megatons

of TNT.

3. The term "bomb" comes from the Greek word "bombein," which means "to make a loud noise."

4. The first successful use of a bomb in warfare was during the Siege of Granada in 1487, when Spanish forces used gunpowder to breach the walls of the city.

5. In World War II, the Germans developed a bomb called the "bouncing bomb," which was designed to skip across water and destroy dams.

6. The "Mother of All Bombs" (MOAB) is the largest non-nuclear bomb in the world, with a yield of 11 tons of TNT, and was developed by the U.S. military.

7. The U.S. dropped atomic bombs on the Japanese cities of Hiroshima and Nagasaki in 1945, killing an estimated 200,000 people and bringing an end to World War II.

8. In 2007, a group of thieves stole a truck containing a large amount of explosives in Mexico City, and accidentally set them off, causing a massive explosion that killed 37 people.

9. The world's first suicide bombing is believed to have been carried out by a Tamil Tiger militant in Sri Lanka in 1980.

10. In 1979, a group of anti-apartheid activists detonated a bomb at a fuel depot near Johannesburg, South Africa, causing a massive explosion that killed one person and injured dozens more.

11. The Oklahoma City bombing in 1995 was the deadliest terrorist attack on U.S. soil prior to the 9/11 attacks, killing 168 people and injuring hundreds

more.

12. In 2002, a bomb-laden fishing boat was used to attack
     a French oil tanker off the coast of Yemen, causing a
     massive explosion that killed one crew member and
     injured several others.

13. The first recorded use of the term "pipe bomb" was in
     1904, when a man named James G. Gifford used one
     to try to blow up his former employer's house.

14. The U.S. government has a program called the "Nuclear
     Emergency Support Team," which is responsible for
     responding to nuclear and radiological emergencies.

15. In 1985, a bomb exploded on board Air India Flight
     182, killing all 329 people on board, making it the
     deadliest terrorist attack in Canadian history.

16. In 2004, a series of bombs exploded on commuter
     trains in Madrid, Spain, killing 191 people and injuring
     over 2,000 others.

17. The largest bomb ever built was the Soviet Union's
     "Tsar Bomba," which had a yield of 50 megatons of
     TNT and weighed over 27,000 pounds.

18. In 2017, a bomb was detonated at an Ariana Grande
     concert in Manchester, England, killing 22 people and
     injuring over 500 others.

19. The U.S. government has a program called the "Bomb
     Squad," which is responsible for disposing of and
     neutralizing explosives.

20. In 2013, two brothers set off two bombs at the Boston
     Marathon, killing three people and injuring hundreds
     more.

<u>Strange facts about the See</u>

1. The Great Barrier Reef is the world's largest living structure and can be seen from outer space.
2. The deepest part of the ocean is the Challenger Deep, located in the Mariana Trench in the western Pacific Ocean, which is over 36,000 feet deep.
3. The world's largest creature, the blue whale, lives in the ocean and can grow up to 100 feet long and weigh over 200 tons.

4. The ocean covers over 70% of the Earth's surface, but only about 5% of it has been explored by humans.

5. The sea level has risen by about 8 inches since 1880, and is expected to rise another 1 to 4 feet by the end of the century due to climate change.

6. The largest waves ever recorded were over 100 feet tall and occurred in the North Atlantic Ocean.

7. The ocean contains more than 20 million tons of gold, but it is too dispersed to be economically recoverable.

8. Jellyfish are not actually fish, but are instead classified as invertebrates.

9. The longest mountain range in the world is located under the ocean, and is called the Mid-Atlantic Ridge.

10. Some types of fish, such as the clownfish, are able to change their gender depending on environmental factors.

11. The ocean is home to some of the world's oldest living organisms, including deep sea sponges that can live for thousands of years.

12. Sea otters hold hands while they sleep to keep from drifting away from each other.

13. The first successful submarine was built by American inventor John Philip Holland in 1898.

14. The ocean contains over 20 million tons of unexploded bombs, chemical weapons, and other hazardous materials dumped during and after World War II.

15. The longest recorded migration by a marine animal was made by a leatherback sea turtle, which swam over 12,000 miles from Indonesia to the coast of Oregon.

16. The ocean is home to some of the world's most

venomous creatures, including box jellyfish, cone snails, and stonefish.

17. The sea is so salty because it contains dissolved minerals and salts that are carried by rivers and streams from land to the ocean.

18. Some types of sharks, such as the Greenland shark, can live for over 400 years, making them some of the longest-lived vertebrates on Earth.

19. The first underwater tunnel was built in 1843 beneath the Thames River in London, England.

20. The ocean is so vast that if Mount Everest, the highest point on Earth, were placed in the Mariana Trench, the deepest part of the ocean, it would still be covered by over a mile of water.

<u>Strange facts about Living Organism's</u>

1. The largest living organism on Earth is a fungus in Oregon that covers an area of over 2,200 acres.
2. The blue whale is the largest animal on Earth and has a heart the size of a car.
3. The common housefly hums in the key of F.
4. A single mature oak tree can release up to 50,000 acorns in one year.
5. The shortest living animal on Earth is the Mayfly, which lives for only a few hours.

6. Some species of bamboo can grow up to 91 cm (36 inches) in just one day.

7. The male seahorse is the only animal in the world that gives birth to its young.

8. The electric eel can discharge up to 600 volts of electricity, which is enough to stun prey and defend itself from predators.

9. The tongue of a blue whale can weigh as much as an elephant.

10. The caterpillar of the gypsy moth can consume up to 86,000 times its body weight in a single day.

11. The lifespan of a taste bud is only 10 days.

12. The blue-ringed octopus is one of the most venomous animals on Earth, and its venom can cause paralysis and death within minutes.

13. The weight of all the ants in the world is roughly equal to the weight of all the humans.

14. The mimic octopus can mimic the shape, color, and movement of over 15 different marine animals.

15. The star-nosed mole has 22 tentacles on its snout that it uses to sense its surroundings and locate prey.

16. The average lifespan of a taste bud is only 10 days.

17. Some species of sea cucumber can expel their internal organs as a defense mechanism, and later regenerate them.

18. The bombardier beetle can spray a boiling hot and toxic liquid from its abdomen to defend itself against predators.

19. The eyes of some species of dragonfly have up to 30,000 lenses, allowing them to see in all directions at

once.

20. The tardigrade, also known as the water bear, is an eight-legged micro-animal that can survive extreme conditions such as extreme heat, cold, radiation, and even the vacuum of space.

<u>Strange facts about Cats</u>

1. There is a Japanese island where cats outnumber humans by six to one.
2. A group of cats is called a clowder.
3. Cats have more than 20 muscles in their ears, which help them to hear and locate sounds more accurately.
4. Cats can make over 100 different vocal sounds.
5. The world's richest cat, Blackie, inherited over $12

million from his wealthy owner in 1988.

6. Cats are the only known domesticated animal that cannot taste sweetness.

7. A cat's sense of smell is 14 times stronger than a human's.

8. A cat's whiskers are highly sensitive and are used to determine whether or not they can fit through a tight space.

9. The oldest known cat breed is the Egyptian Mau, which has been around for over 3,000 years.

10. Cats spend up to one-third of their waking hours grooming themselves.

11. The world's longest cat was a Maine Coon named Stewie, who measured 48.5 inches from nose to tail.

12. Cats can jump up to six times their body length in a single bound.

13. The scientific name for the domestic cat is Felis catus.

14. Cats are able to purr at a frequency that promotes healing and bone growth.

15. The oldest cat on record was named Creme Puff, who lived to be 38 years old.

16. In ancient Egypt, cats were considered sacred animals and were worshipped as such.

17. Cats have a special reflective layer in their eyes called the tapetum lucidum, which allows them to see better in low-light conditions.

18. A cat's tongue is covered in tiny barbs called papillae, which help them to groom themselves more efficiently.

19. The world's largest cat was a tiger that weighed over 1,000 pounds.

20. The Siamese cat is one of the few cat breeds that has crossed eyes as a natural trait.

<u>Strange facts about Waterfalls</u>

1. The highest waterfall in the world, Angel Falls in Venezuela, is so high that the water turns to mist before it reaches the bottom.

2. The tallest waterfall in North America is Yosemite Falls

in California, which drops 2,425 feet.

3. The widest waterfall in the world is Khone Phapheng Falls on the Mekong River in Laos, which is over 35,000 feet wide.

4. The longest waterfall in the world is the Boyoma Falls on the Congo River in Africa, which stretches for over 60 miles.

5. The largest waterfall in terms of water volume is the Victoria Falls on the Zambezi River in Africa, which can reach a flow rate of over 1 million liters per second during the wet season.

6. The highest year-round waterfall in the world is Gocta Cataracts in Peru, which drops 2,531 feet.

7. The tallest waterfall in Europe is the Krimmler Waterfall in Austria, which drops 1,247 feet.

8. The tallest waterfall in Asia is the Jog Falls in India, which drops 829 feet.

9. The tallest waterfall in Australia is the Wallaman Falls in Queensland, which drops 984 feet.

10. The tallest waterfall in South America (excluding Angel Falls) is the Salto del Guairá in Paraguay, which drops 131 feet.

11. The tallest waterfall in Antarctica is the Blood Falls, which is not actually a waterfall, but a red outflow of saltwater from an underground lake.

12. The tallest waterfall in the United States is the Ribbon Falls in California, which drops 1,612 feet.

13. The tallest waterfall in Canada is the Della Falls in British Columbia, which drops 1,444 feet.

14. The tallest waterfall in Africa (excluding Victoria Falls)

is the Tugela Falls in South Africa, which drops 3,110 feet.

15. The tallest waterfall in Oceania (excluding Australia) is the Sutherland Falls in New Zealand, which drops 1,904 feet.

16. The tallest waterfall in Central America is the San Ramon Waterfall in Costa Rica, which drops 350 feet.

17. The tallest waterfall in the Caribbean is the El Limón Waterfall in the Dominican Republic, which drops 131 feet.

18. The tallest waterfall in the Middle East is the Shirabad Waterfall in Iran, which drops 180 feet.

19. The tallest waterfall in Southeast Asia is the Langkawi Waterfall in Malaysia, which drops 500 feet.

20. The tallest waterfall in Russia is the Kivach Falls, which drops 98 feet.

<u>Strange facts about Humans lifting Things</u>

1. The strongest human muscle in proportion to its size is the tongue.
2. The human heart can create enough pressure to squirt blood up to 30 feet away.
3. The average person produces enough saliva in their lifetime to fill two swimming pools.
4. The human body can withstand more G-force than a

rocket launch.

5. The world record for the longest time holding a 10-pound weight in each hand is over 30 minutes.

6. The world record for the heaviest weight lifted with just one finger is over 500 pounds.

7. The world record for the heaviest weight ever lifted by a human being using only their teeth is over 1,000 pounds.

8. The world record for the heaviest weight ever lifted by a human being with their hair is over 200 pounds.

9. The world record for the heaviest weight ever lifted by a human being with their ear is over 100 pounds.

10. The world record for the heaviest weight ever lifted by a human being with their nose is over 1,000 pounds.

11. The world record for the most weight lifted with one finger in 30 seconds is over 1,000 pounds.

12. The world record for the most weight lifted with the ear in 30 seconds is over 200 pounds.

13. The world record for the most weight lifted with the nose in 30 seconds is over 1,000 pounds.

14. The world record for the most weight lifted with the teeth in 30 seconds is over 1,100 pounds.

15. The world record for the most weight lifted with the hair in 30 seconds is over 40 pounds.

16. The world record for the most weight lifted with the eyelids is over 4 pounds.

17. The world record for the most weight lifted with the tongue is over 28 pounds.

18. The world record for the most weight lifted with the feet while in a handstand is over 300 pounds.

19. The world record for the most weight lifted with the legs while standing on the hands is over 600 pounds.

20. The world record for the most weight lifted with the buttocks is over 700 pounds.

Strange facts about Weddings

1. The longest wedding veil ever made was over 6,000 feet long.
2. In South Korea, it is traditional for the groom to give his mother-in-law a pair of live ducks or geese as a symbol of fidelity.
3. In Congo, it is customary for the bride and groom to avoid smiling during the wedding ceremony.
4. The tradition of carrying the bride over the threshold

comes from the belief that evil spirits lived in the ground, and carrying the bride would protect her from them.

5. In some cultures, including Greece and Spain, the groom wears his wedding ring on his right hand instead of his left.

6. In traditional Hindu weddings, the bride and groom exchange flower garlands as a symbol of their acceptance of each other.

7. In Mexico, it is traditional for the couple to be showered with red beads and flowers after the wedding ceremony.

8. In Scotland, it is traditional for the bride and groom to be "piped" out of the ceremony with bagpipes playing.

9. In ancient Rome, brides carried a bouquet of herbs, such as garlic and rosemary, to ward off evil spirits.

10. In Denmark, it is traditional for the bride and groom to be pelted with cinnamon and pepper when they leave the ceremony.

11. In some parts of China, it is traditional for the bride to wear a red dress instead of a white one.

12. In Sweden, it is traditional for the bride to wear a crown of myrtle leaves, which symbolizes love and fertility.

13. In Ethiopia, it is traditional for the groom to give the bride's family a dowry of cows or goats.

14. In Germany, it is traditional for the bride and groom to saw a log in half together as a symbol of their teamwork.

15. In some cultures, including Hindu and Chinese, rain

on the wedding day is considered good luck.

16. In the Netherlands, it is traditional for the bride and groom to plant lilies-of-the-valley together after the wedding ceremony.

17. In ancient Egypt, wedding rings were made of braided reeds or hemp, and were worn on the fourth finger of the left hand because it was believed that a vein in that finger led directly to the heart.

18. In Italy, it is traditional for the groom to carry a small piece of iron in his pocket on the wedding day to ward off evil spirits.

19. In some cultures, including Nigerian and Moroccan, the bride and groom are crowned with flowers and sit on a throne during the wedding ceremony.

20. In some parts of India, it is traditional for the bride and groom to paint their hands and feet with henna in intricate designs as a symbol of their love and commitment.

Strange facts about the Driest places

1. The McMurdo Dry Valleys in Antarctica are the driest non-polar desert on Earth.
2. The Danakil Depression in Ethiopia is one of the hottest and driest places on Earth, with temperatures that can reach up to 145°F (63°C).
3. Death Valley in California, USA, is the hottest and driest place in North America, with an average temperature of 115°F (46°C).

4. The Namib Desert in Namibia is one of the oldest and driest deserts in the world, with some areas receiving less than 2 inches of rain per year.
5. The Sonoran Desert in North America is the wettest and most biologically diverse desert in the world.
6. The Rub' al Khali (Empty Quarter) in Saudi Arabia is the largest contiguous sand desert in the world.
7. The Gobi Desert, which spans China and Mongolia, is the fifth-largest desert in the world and is known for its extreme temperature fluctuations.
8. The Thar Desert in India and Pakistan is the seventh-largest desert in the world and is home to several unique species of wildlife.
9. The Nubian Desert in northeastern Africa is one of the driest and most inhospitable deserts in the world, with an average annual rainfall of less than 1 inch.
10. The Simpson Desert in Australia is the fourth-largest desert in the country and is home to over 180 species of birds.
11. The Karoo Desert in South Africa is one of the most geologically diverse deserts in the world.
12. The Taklamakan Desert in China is the second-largest shifting sand desert in the world.
13. The Negev Desert in Israel is the only desert in the world with a year-round resident population of over 1 million people.
14. The Dasht-e Lut in Iran is one of the driest and hottest places on Earth, with temperatures that can reach up to 159°F (71°C).
15. The Kalahari Desert in Southern Africa is home to

several indigenous tribes and is known for its vast sand dunes and unique wildlife.

16. The Ténéré Desert in the Sahara Desert is one of the most remote and least inhabited regions on Earth.

17. The Salar de Uyuni in Bolivia is the largest salt flat in the world and is one of the driest places on Earth.

18. The Qattara Depression in Egypt is one of the lowest and driest places on Earth, with an average annual rainfall of less than half an inch.

19. The Leh and Ladakh deserts in India are the highest deserts in the world, with some areas located over 10,000 feet above sea level.

20. The Arctic and Antarctic are technically classified as deserts due to their low levels of precipitation.

<u>Strange facts about Snow</u>

1. Snowflakes can take up to 2 hours to fall from the clouds to the ground.
2. The snowiest city in the world is Aomori City in Japan, which receives an average of 312 inches of snowfall per year.
3. The Inuit have over 50 words to describe snow, depending on the texture, shape, and other properties.
4. The tallest snowman ever built was over 113 feet tall

and was constructed in Maine in 2008.

5. Snow is not actually white, but clear. The crystals scatter light in all directions, making it appear white.

6. It is possible to make ice cream out of snow by mixing it with condensed milk and flavorings.

7. The world's largest snowball fight involved over 7,000 participants and was held in Saskatoon, Canada in 2016.

8. The world record for the most snow angels made in one place is 8,962 and was set in Bismarck, North Dakota in 2007.

9. The largest snowflake ever recorded was 15 inches wide and 8 inches thick.

10. Snow can act as a natural sound absorber, making everything seem quieter during a snowfall.

11. The Russian language has two different words for snow: "снег" (sneg) for falling snow and "снежок" (snezhok) for a snowball.

12. The world's largest snow maze is located in Warren, Vermont and covers over 10,000 square feet.

13. The world's largest snow fort was built in Canada and was over 27 feet tall and 80 feet wide.

14. Snow can be used as insulation in igloos and can keep the inside temperature above freezing even when it's -40 degrees outside.

15. The city of Sapporo, Japan holds an annual snow festival featuring massive ice sculptures and snow statues.

16. The snowiest place in the United States is Mount Baker in Washington state, which holds the record for

the most snowfall in a single season with 1,140 inches.

17. The largest snowflake cluster ever recorded fell in Montana in 1887 and measured 15 inches wide and 8 inches thick.

18. The coldest temperature ever recorded on Earth was -128.6 degrees Fahrenheit in Antarctica in 1983.

19. The word "blizzard" comes from the Old Norse word "blizzr," meaning "a biting wind."

20. In the early 1900s, it was a common practice to collect snow in the winter and store it in ice houses to be used as a source of refrigeration during the summer months.

<u>Strange facts about Deep Places</u>

1. The deepest part of the ocean, the Mariana Trench, is 36,070 feet (10,994 meters) deep.
2. The pressure at the bottom of the Mariana Trench is over 8 tons per square inch.
3. The Mariana Trench is located in the western Pacific Ocean, near the Mariana Islands.
4. In 2012, filmmaker James Cameron became the first person to solo dive to the bottom of the Mariana

Trench.

5. The Kola Superdeep Borehole in Russia is the deepest hole ever dug by humans, reaching a depth of 7.5 miles (12 kilometers).

6. The temperature at the bottom of the Kola Superdeep Borehole reached 356 degrees Fahrenheit (180 degrees Celsius).

7. The Hranice Abyss in the Czech Republic is the deepest flooded freshwater abyss in the world, reaching a depth of 1,325 feet (404 meters).

8. The Devil's Sinkhole in Texas is a vertical cave that drops down 400 feet (122 meters).

9. The Cenote Angelita in Mexico is a deep sinkhole that contains a layer of hydrogen sulfide gas at a depth of 100 feet (30 meters).

10. The Black Sea has a layer of hydrogen sulfide at a depth of 200 feet (60 meters), which makes it difficult for marine life to survive below that depth.

11. The Grand Canyon in Arizona is one of the deepest canyons in the world, with a maximum depth of 6,093 feet (1,857 meters).

12. The La Brea Tar Pits in Los Angeles, California contain a lake of asphalt that reaches a depth of 16 feet (5 meters).

13. The deepest point in Antarctica, the Bentley Subglacial Trench, reaches a depth of 8,383 feet (2,555 meters).

14. The Dead Sea, which is located between Jordan and Israel, is the lowest point on Earth, with a surface elevation of 1,388 feet (423 meters) below sea level.

15. The Maldives, a chain of islands in the Indian Ocean,

has an average elevation of only 5 feet (1.5 meters) above sea level.

16. Lake Baikal in Russia is the deepest freshwater lake in the world, with a maximum depth of 5,387 feet (1,642 meters).

17. The world's largest cave, Son Doong Cave in Vietnam, reaches a depth of over 650 feet (200 meters).

18. The Blue Hole in Belize is a popular diving spot that reaches a depth of 407 feet (124 meters).

19. The Pozzo del Merro in Italy is the deepest underwater vertical cave in the world, reaching a depth of 1,286 feet (392 meters).

20. The Deepsea Challenger, a submersible designed to explore the deepest parts of the ocean, reached a depth of 35,787 feet (10,908 meters) during a dive in 2012.

<u>Strange facts about Fruit and vegetables</u>

1. The world's spiciest pepper is the Carolina Reaper, which measures over 2.2 million on the Scoville heat scale.
2. Apples float in water because they are 25% air.
3. The world's most expensive mushroom, the white truffle, can sell for up to $3,000 per pound.
4. The world's largest avocado weighed over 5 pounds.

5. Honey never spoils, and it has been found in ancient Egyptian tombs still edible after thousands of years.
6. Durian, a fruit popular in Southeast Asia, is so pungent that it is banned on public transportation in some countries.
7. The world's most expensive coffee, Kopi Luwak, is made from beans that have been eaten and excreted by a civet.
8. The world's largest grapefruit weighed over 18 pounds.
9. The world's largest watermelon weighed over 350 pounds.
10. Potatoes were the first vegetable grown in space.
11. The world's largest strawberry was over 8 inches long and weighed over 250 grams.
12. The world's largest carrot was over 19 feet long and weighed over 22 pounds.
13. The world's largest tomato plant grew over 65 feet tall and produced over 32,000 tomatoes.
14. Chocolate was once used as currency in ancient civilizations like the Mayans and Aztecs.
15. The world's largest sweet potato weighed over 81 pounds.
16. The world's most expensive fruit is the Japanese Yubari melon, which can sell for up to $20,000 per pair.
17. The world's largest onion weighed over 18 pounds.
18. The world's largest garlic bulb weighed over 5 pounds.
19. The world's most expensive spice is saffron, which can cost up to $10,000 per pound.
20. The world's largest corn maze covers over 60 acres.

<u>Strange facts about Small Mammals</u>

1. The bumblebee bat, also known as Kitti's hog-nosed bat, is the world's smallest mammal, weighing less than a penny.
2. A group of hedgehogs is called a prickle.
3. Shrews have a very high metabolism and can eat up to three times their own body weight in a day.
4. The platypus is one of the few mammals that lay eggs

instead of giving birth to live young.

5. Flying squirrels can glide through the air for up to 300 feet.
6. A group of ferrets is called a business.
7. The star-nosed mole has 22 fleshy tentacles around its nose that it uses to feel around for food.
8. Hamsters have cheeks that can stretch to about twice the size of their head, allowing them to carry food and bedding back to their nests.
9. The pygmy jerboa, a small rodent found in Asia, can jump up to six feet in a single bound.
10. A baby kangaroo is called a joey.
11. The Tasmanian devil is the world's largest carnivorous marsupial.
12. A group of otters is called a romp.
13. The naked mole-rat is the only known mammal to live in a eusocial society, similar to that of ants or bees.
14. The common mole can dig a tunnel up to 300 feet long in just one night.
15. The smallest primate in the world is the pygmy marmoset, which can fit in the palm of a human hand.
16. A group of meerkats is called a mob.
17. The aye-aye, a type of lemur found in Madagascar, has a long, thin middle finger that it uses to extract insects from tree bark.
18. The kangaroo rat can go its entire life without drinking water, getting all the moisture it needs from the seeds it eats.
19. A group of rabbits is called a herd or a colony.
20. The smallest rodent in the world is the pygmy jerboa,

which measures just 1.3 inches long.

Strange facts about Computers and the Web

1. The first computer mouse was made of wood.
2. The first hard drive was made in 1979 and could only hold 5MB of data.
3. The first computer virus was created in 1983 and was called the "Elk Cloner."
4. The QWERTY keyboard layout was designed in the 1870s to prevent typewriter keys from jamming.
5. The first smartphone, IBM's Simon, was released in

1993.

6. The world's first computer programmer was Ada Lovelace, who wrote programs for Charles Babbage's Analytical Engine in the 1840s.

7. The first computer game, Spacewar!, was created in 1962.

8. The first digital camera was created in 1975 and weighed 8 pounds.

9. The first website was created in 1991 by Tim Berners-Lee.

10. The first emoticon, :-) was used in an email in 1979.

11. The first banner ad appeared on the internet in 1994.

12. The first computer animation was created in 1962 by John Whitney Sr.

13. The first Wi-Fi network was developed in 1991.

14. The first hard drive was invented in 1956 and was the size of a refrigerator.

15. The first computer game console, the Magnavox Odyssey, was released in 1972.

16. The first webcam was invented in 1991 at Cambridge University to monitor a coffee pot.

17. The first spam email was sent in 1978 to 393 people.

18. The first computer voice recognition program was created in 1952.

19. The first graphical web browser was developed in 1993 and was called Mosaic.

20. The first computer virus to cause widespread damage was the "Melissa" virus in 1999.

<u>Strange facts about Swimming Pools</u>

1. The first swimming pool to use a water filtration system was built in 1910 in Texas.
2. The largest indoor swimming pool is located in Japan and is 300 meters long, 100 meters wide, and 38 meters deep.
3. The deepest swimming pool in the world is the Y-40 Deep Joy in Italy, which has a depth of 42 meters (138 feet).

4. The largest swimming pool in the world by water volume is the San Alfonso del Mar seawater pool in Chile, which holds over 66 million gallons of water.
5. The world's first infinity pool was built in 1979 on the island of Maui, Hawaii.
6. The fastest swimmer in the world is currently Cesar Cielo from Brazil, who holds the world record in the 50-meter freestyle.
7. The largest hot spring pool in the world is the Glenwood Hot Springs Pool in Colorado, which is over two city blocks long.
8. The highest swimming pool in the world is located on the 118th floor of the Ritz-Carlton hotel in Hong Kong.
9. The world's first natural swimming pool was built in 1984 in Austria and uses plants and natural filters instead of chlorine.
10. The smallest swimming pool in the world is located in the backyard of a house in the United Kingdom and is just 2.6 meters long.
11. The longest continuous swim ever recorded was 177 hours and 10 minutes, set by Martin Strel in 2007 in a pool in Slovenia.
12. The first above-ground swimming pool was patented in 1916 and was made from galvanized steel.
13. The world's largest swimming lesson was held in 2019 and involved over 50,000 participants across 27 countries.
14. The first swimming pool to have underwater windows was built in the 1930s in California.

15. The world's oldest public swimming pool is the Great Bath in Pakistan, which dates back over 5,000 years.
16. The first Olympic swimming event for women was held in 1912 in Stockholm, Sweden.
17. The world's largest swimming pool complex is located in Tokyo, Japan and consists of 21 different pools.
18. The first heated indoor swimming pool was built in 1869 in England.
19. The world's first wave pool was built in 1927 in Munich, Germany and used compressed air to create waves.
20. The largest indoor wave pool is located in Edmonton, Canada and covers an area of 40,000 square feet.

<u>Strange facts about Volcanos</u>

1. The word "volcano" comes from the name of the
   Roman god of fire, Vulcan.
2. There are approximately 1,500 active volcanoes around
   the world.
3. The largest volcano in the solar system is on Mars, and
   it is called Olympus Mons.
4. Volcanic ash can travel as far as 20 miles away from the
   eruption site.

5. The eruption of Mount Vesuvius in 79 AD buried the city of Pompeii in Italy.

6. The eruption of Mount Tambora in 1815 was the largest volcanic eruption in recorded history.

7. The Hawaiian Islands were formed by underwater volcanic eruptions.

8. There is a volcanic lake in Cameroon called Lake Nyos that caused the deaths of over 1,700 people in 1986 due to a carbon dioxide eruption.

9. The world's most active volcano is Kilauea, located on the Big Island of Hawaii.

10. A volcanic eruption can cause lightning to occur within the ash clouds.

11. The island of Iceland was formed entirely by volcanic eruptions.

12. The term "lava" comes from the Italian word for "stream."

13. Volcanic eruptions can lead to the formation of new land masses, such as the island of Surtsey off the coast of Iceland.

14. The world's highest volcano is Ojos del Salado, located on the border of Chile and Argentina.

15. In 1783, the eruption of Laki in Iceland caused a global temperature decrease and famine due to the release of sulfur dioxide into the atmosphere.

16. The Ring of Fire is a region around the Pacific Ocean where a large number of volcanic eruptions and earthquakes occur.

17. The island of Krakatoa in Indonesia had a massive eruption in 1883 that could be heard from over 3,000

miles away.

18. The Roman city of Herculaneum was destroyed by the eruption of Mount Vesuvius in 79 AD, but the city of Pompeii was actually buried by the ash and pumice.

19. In 1980, the eruption of Mount St. Helens in Washington State was the deadliest and most economically destructive volcanic event in the history of the United States.

20. The blue lava seen in Kawah Ijen volcano in Indonesia is caused by the combustion of sulfuric gases.

ABOUT THE AUTHOR

KOBUS FOURIE IS AN ardent seeker of knowledge, driven by an insatiable curiosity that permeates every aspect of his life. With an unwavering passion for uncovering the hidden intricacies of the world, he has devoted years to delving into the realms of strange and fascinating facts. Drawing from a vast array of subjects, Kobus has cultivated a deep understanding of the peculiar and extraordinary that exists within our reality.

From an early age, Kobus's inquisitive nature propelled him on a journey of discovery, constantly seeking out the obscure and the remarkable. His unquenchable thirst for knowledge has been the catalyst for his tireless research and exploration, leading him to gather a wealth of captivating information that he eagerly shares with others. In particular, he finds immense joy in imparting this wisdom to his two children, instilling in them a love for the intriguing world of facts that surrounds us.

While the pursuit of knowledge consumes much of Kobus's time, he also cherishes moments spent with his family, relishing in the simple pleasures of togetherness. Nature beckons him outdoors, where he finds solace and inspiration amidst the beauty of the natural world. Additionally, he finds creative expression in the kitchen, constantly experimenting with new recipes that tantalize both the taste buds and the imagination.

Through this book of strange facts, Kobus endeavors to share his boundless enthusiasm for knowledge with readers of all ages. He aspires to ignite the spark of curiosity within each individual, fostering a sense of wonder and a desire to explore the endless wonders that lie just beneath the surface of our everyday lives. By delving into the captivating world of peculiar facts, he hopes to inspire a lifelong love for learning and an unwavering appreciation for the fascinating intricacies that abound in our extraordinary world.

With a genuine dedication to the pursuit of knowledge and a profound belief in the transformative power of curiosity, Kobus Fourie invites readers to embark on a remarkable journey through the strange, the enigmatic, and the awe-inspiring.

Don't miss out!

Visit the website below and you can sign up to receive emails whenever Kobus Fourie publishes a new book. There's no charge and no obligation.

https://books2read.com/r/B-A-KVXX-MOLIC

BOOKS2READ

Connecting independent readers to independent writers.